D0395977

TWILIGHT OF THE IDOLS

TWILIGHT OF THE IDOLS
RECOLLECTIONS OF A LOST YUGOSLAVIA

AN ESSAY BY
ALEŠ DEBELJAK

TRANSLATED FROM THE SLOVENIAN BY
MICHAEL BIGGINS

PHOTOGRAPHS BY
ELIZABETH RAPPAPORT

WHITE PINE PRESS

Publication of this book was made possible,
in part, by grants from
the National Endowment for the Arts,
the New York State Council on the Arts,
and the Trubar Foundation.

Cover photograph by Elizabeth Rappaport

Author photograph by Jani Štraus

Book design by Elaine LaMattina

Manufactured in the United States of America

ISBN 1-877727-51-2

9 8 7 6 5 4 3 2 1

Published by
White Pine Press
10 Village Square
Fredonia, New York 14063

TWILIGHT OF THE IDOLS

Contents

Who Now Remembers Vukovar?
11

Brush Me With Your Knee Beneath the Table
45

The Photographs
77

Map
79

The Author
81

The Photographer
83

The Translator
85

For Erica, who wants to understand

I.

Who Now Remembers Vukovar?

All the signs of the times suggest that "celebration of diversity" has become the official by-word of the end of the millenium. One doesn't have to look far for evidence that this off-shoot of traditional liberal thought is blossoming in the heart of contemporary world culture. Even a casual observer could notice the variety of forms assumed by this enchanting but never fully realized formula for social and political co-existence.

On the glossy pages of fashion magazines or on the street corners of Berlin, New York, and Paris you can see this "celebration of diversity" in the exchange of a business suit for a sari or of worn-out hippie rags for the elegant cut of the *alta moda di Versace*. The same phrase appears on the rustling pages of the morning papers, where columnists vie for our attention with television's sweet, soporific images of distant lands and exotic foreigners that threaten to lure us away from what Hegel referred to as the "morning prayers of the bourgeoisie."

These strangers really bear no resemblance at all to us as we hold sway — remote control switch in hand — over the last refuge of our privacy. They're different from us, these refugees and nomads, migrant workers and displaced persons. As they flee repression and poverty, they pay the high price of diversity at every Western border they try to cross.

"Diversity is a resource that egalitarianism of stomachs and minds threatens to destroy," political leaders proclaim from their lecterns before they withdraw to dine in the towers of diplomatic and economic power. The imperial wisdom of Downing Street, the White House, and the Quai d'Orsay has had these towers built without windows for a reason: so that "the free world's leaders" don't accidentally notice that the Pilate-like washing of their hands has led to political vivisections which turned neighbors' yards into front lines of homicidal frenzy.

The black, white, yellow, and red faces smiling at us in youthful embarrassment from advertisements for the United Colors of Benetton seem to be speaking the same slogan. Diversity — that promise of growing hope in a catastrophic world where hope has become a luxury of the select few. Diversity — that slender reed of hope onto which women, gays, lesbians, blacks, Turkish workers in Germany, Moroccans and Algerians in France, Native Americans, Kurds and Tibetans, Tamils and Lithuanians have all seized. Maybe, they think, the reed of diversity will allow them to breathe beneath the troubled surface of modern societies, which until yesterday seemed homogeneous but whose form and substance are changing faster than their frightened members are able to admit.

Within the walls of intellectual centers throughout Western Europe and North America, the high priests of enlightenment spread the word of a new philosophy of

diversity, tolerance, and multiculturalism. These are the most recent by-words for co-existence in a complex, interdependent society where individuals are no longer compelled to submit to the effects of the American melting pot and its watered-down European imitations.

During the heroic age of worldwide emigration of the nineteenth century, diverse cultures, religions, and identities intermingled to the point of becoming indistinguishable from one another. For the sake of their own social advancement, minority groups were obliged to speak the language of some dominant culture. Today, so say the experts, we can enjoy the benefits of so-called post-modern society, which more closely resembles a salad bowl. Its advantage is that we can see each of the primary ingredients and not worry about them vanishing in the intermingling that defines the overall taste.

Progressive and inspirational ideas, to be sure.

But those of us who were born in the land of mass political rallies and brilliant communist rhetoric used by Tito to seduce the drawing-room leftists of Europe and America; those of us who as schoolchildren were lined up along the parade routes of the former Yugoslav federation to wave flags at the great Marshal as he rode past in glory; those of us who watched dumbfounded as the Serbian masses orgiastically observed the six hundredth anniversary of their ancestors' defeat by the Turks on the Plain of Kosovo and Albanian Kosovars, held captive by the Serb-imposed apartheid, didn't dare show their faces on the streets of their own villages and towns; those of us who could observe from close up as pathologically ambitious novelists, self-proclaimed "fathers of the nation," and failed poets traded their pens for machine gun triggers in the powerful belief that this would be a quicker way of convincing the masses that all Serbs must unite within a single state; those of us who looked on in horror as the vengeance of Yugoslavia's flunkies in the school of democracy demolished a real culture of diversity — we were the ones who learned in the hardest way possible that the masses on Europe's periphery, if not in its heart, don't give a damn for reasoned co-existence in a diverse society.

The masses would rather turn to those seductive sirens whose songs they most easily understand. These are the sirens of inherited mythological archetypes, the sirens of tribal tradition. Individuals ingest the words and melodies of these songs with their mothers' milk. Generation after generation absorbs them from the tales their grandfathers spin at evening. The collective memory of any nation clings to the experience of the past, without which there can be no vision of the future.

Let's face it: in times of crisis we're all at least a little inclined to take atavistic refuge in proven survival strategies of the sort that helped our ancestors weather the changing of idols without actually having to change themselves. Isn't the power of collective memory, chaining us to inherited formulas, at its strongest precisely when we face the challenge of new horizons, the collapse of old regimes, the royal road to a more promising future?

This is why collective memory is a two-edged sword: one edge protects the source of security from running dry, while the other prevents members of the society from developing their critical faculties and independence from tradition. A nation adapts itself to the modern paradigm only when it is no longer tribal shamans who determine social behavior but the most capable individuals, who tend to the common good in accordance with reason and popular consensus.

When a nation succeeds in rationally defining its common good, it makes the transition from an undifferentiated community to a structured society, from tradition to modernity. Simultaneously it has to free itself from a cyclical and mythological conception of time, in which the perpetual repetition of the same archetypes obliterates any distinction between yesterday, today, and tomorrow. Only time as an unrepeatable progression — the fleeting, eternally new passage of moments — marks the real birth of modern consciousness. The modern concept of time tells us that past events themselves are no prescription for action in the present but rather an opportunity for critical self-evaluation based on the mistakes of earlier generations.

When a talented individual retreats into the realm of memory, mankind is rewarded with a work of art. When an entire nation surrenders to memory's maelstrom, mankind is faced with a catastrophe. An individual's retreat into memory is the right and privilege of the artist, who pays for the narcissism of his artistic achievement with personal isolation. A collective retreat into the past that is used to justify a bloody present makes others liable for the cost of its chauvinism, placing the debt on the shoulders of those who do not share in the collective memory of the "ethnically pure" nation and are doomed to be its victims.

The immortal aroma of *madeleines* brought Marcel Proust the freedom to turn his rooms on the Boulevard

Saint-Germain into a world where meticulously described metamorphoses of love, jealousy, and artistocratic back-biting could reincarnate a mysterious time and place that would never fade.

For the space of a few pages of Á *la recherche du temps perdu*, Serbian countesses promenade across Parisian parquet floors. The Serbian bourgeoisie's traditional francophilism sent many poets to serve their apprenticeship in the streets and lecture halls of Paris to broaden their aesthetic and political ideas.

At its birth, surrealism found impassioned Serbian disciples in Marko Ristič, Milan Dedinac, and Dušan Matič, who introduced the rules of automatic writing to Belgrade's literary magazines. From today's vantage point, it seems as though their anthology *Impossible* (1930) was already hinting at the parameters of dialogue with foreign cultures. The anthology's title has a prophetic ring, while its forgotten contents reveal a spirit of cosmopolitanism that contemporary fascist Serbia has driven out the front door.

The recollection of *madeleines* eaten in his aunt's salon was enough to propel Proust into labyrinths of the past. The pungent scent of Kosovo peonies suffices to do the same for today's Serbs. According to folk legend this dark red flower grows from the blood of Serbian heroes cut down by Turkish swords in the Battle of Kosovo (1389), an event that cost medieval Serbia its freedom. But instead of once traditional laments for the dead, the Kosovo peony now evokes only the terror with which the Serbs wage their war against Bosnia, pathologically seeking vengeance for defeats suffered over six hundred years ago.

❦ Twilight of the Idols ❦

Word and deed are one and the same only in myths. It should, therefore, be no surprise that the present Serbian elite is engaged in a war of words and weapons to resurrect an archaic mentality, and with it a cultural and national identity. The obsession of the Serbian intellectual, political, and military leadership — not to mention the vast majority of the Serbian populace — with the megalomaniacal dream of a Greater Serbia may well cause the present genocidal war to be perceived as a feat of patriotic greatness. The smoke screen of Serbian *amor patriae* has clouded the vision and fogged the memory of many an outside observer.

Consider this: who now remembers Vukovar? A city on the border between Croatia and Serbia. A city that with its baroque palaces, impoverished aristocracy, and *Sachertorten* represented one of the easternmost outposts of Central European culture. No one remembers it now. Indeed, it's as though many winters had passed since hordes of Serbian paramilitary troops supported by Belgrade leveled that Croatian city, though in fact it happened as recently as November 1991. Not one stone remains atop another now in what used to be a charming provincial town of a hundred thousand inhabitants. "Liberated," according to official Serbian propaganda.

For a horrified, but more than a little bored, "international community" those ruins are nothing more than a "smoked pipe," as a Bosnian acquaintance and fellow writer, who was forced to flee from Sarajevo to Germany with her child, eloquently put it.

The fate of Vukovar is, or at least is likely to be, the fate of Sarajevo. And before long, the awesome ruins of Sarajevo will also have become a "smoked pipe" for

23

the political powers in the West, and then also for the Western public, which is at least a step ahead of its leaders in outrage against Serbia's inexplicable campaign of genocide. That step divides morality from politics, although morality can help us save nothing but our souls. We cannot save the Moslems, the sacrificial lambs of the new world disorder. If any survive, they will be kept in special preserves as a quiet rebuke to mankind — with stress put on the "quiet."

How could it be different? Schoolchildren from all over Europe, upon visiting Dachau, Auschwitz, and Treblinka, remark that their tours through the sites where one race turned another into ashes are more of a "tiresome obligation" than a history lesson. History is, after all, only a lamp on the ship's stern, writes Coleridge. It does not lead forward; it can only show us where we've been. And if we don't look back, we won't even know that much. History's nightmare won't haunt us in that convenient case. Clearly, we're afraid of nightmares, and the anti-fascist and anti-genocidal "never again" that is supposedly a cornerstone of Europe's political conscience has become nothing but an empty slogan repeated dutifully once a year.

After World War II, surviving Jews devoted enormous financial and intellectual resources, not to mention diplomatic and political efforts, to preserving the historical memory of the "final solution" and the catastrophic consequences of national socialism. In spite of all of the trials in Jerusalem, the "banality of evil," the museums and exhibits, the plethora of newspaper and magazine articles, books, university courses, Nazi hunters, and Elie Wiesel's tales of suffering, it is hard to rid oneself of the feeling that the Holocaust does not have a real place in the European conscience. If it did, the Serbian leadership would not be rewarded for its *argumentum baculinum,* big stick, politics with more and more conquered territory.

I can hear voices raised in skeptical opposition. Of course, I also know the objections. Politics is not ethics. Geostrategical interests, deranged tribalism, a land with no oil, fear of the economic costs, the distasteful thought of tow-headed boys from Iowa and Provence lying dead in the distant Balkans. Obviously, we all know these objections by heart. Just as obvious, however, is the fact that we will have to learn to live with new values and ideals in the coming century, for our century died in Sarajevo.

I am deeply convinced that each of us must do the utmost to insure that this Balkan genocide does not pass into oblivion. The Western powers that allowed the genocide to happen will pressure particularly members of the one-time Yugoslav federation to re-open "relations" with the Serbian regime, with its leaders, economists, writers, and artists, all in the name of forgetting (and forgiving). I can understand that commerce is unavoidable; soon after 1945, the Allies re-opened trade with a de-nazified Germany. In a world of economic interdependence, these contacts are inevitable. However, "relations" with intellectuals, writers, and scholars who stood at the crib of Serbian national socialism and continue to actively or passively support it even today are not.

The longing for a bigger market, a broader audience, a more numerous readership: all of these are legitimate feelings on the part of former Yugoslavs. Yet these feelings cannot help but be rooted in the past. Today, there is an enormous gulf between the past and the present, filled to its edges with mutilated corpses from Erdut, Dalj, Vukovar, Sarajevo, Goražade, Žepa, and countless other anonymous towns throughout Bosnia and Croatia. To justify the hundreds of thousands of dead, the incessant rattlers of the glorious Serbian military tradition also have to sacrifice any critical stance toward history.

With the drafting of the infamous *Memorandum of the Serbian Academy of Arts and Sciences* in 1986, Serbian history — rich with wonderful folk songs, dances, and architecture — metastasized on the maps of the communist generals in Belgrade into a Serbian *Drang nach Westen*, "push toward the West."

In this document, Serbian academics, members of the highest and most authoritative Serbian intellectual institution, articulated a political and pseudo-historical justification, later skillfully exploited by Milosevic, for the bloody Serbian war of aggression. *The Memorandum,* though unfinished, had a powerful impact on the population when, after having circulated for some time clandestinely, it emerged in public. Its primary focus was the claim that Serbia had been routinely cheated of territories in past wars. This mythological interpretation of facts subsequently functioned as the principal source of Serbia's current appetite for foreign lands.

"What Serbs gain in war, they lose in peace" was one of the astoundingly popular slogans. It carried irrational power of persuasion not only because of the historical frustrations to which it gave voice, but first and foremost because it was penned by the most celebrated modern Serbian novelist, a revered "patriarch of the

nation," and a short-term president of Milosevic's rump Yugoslavia, Dobrica Cosic.

Suggesting that Serbs are good warriors but poor citizens, Cosic's numerous novels and the *Memorandum* and the massive ideological avalanche it unleashed, converged on one demand: all Serbs must live in one country! This implied a unification of three distinct groups. Serbian minorities in Croatia, descendants of refugees who fled the army of the Ottoman Empire in the 16th and 17th centuries and who were later appointed soldiers on the southeastern Austrian *military frontier* under the House of Hapsburg, must be at any cost united with Serbia proper and with indigenous Serbian enclaves in Bosnia. Here, an Orthodox Serb population has lived for centuries relatively peacefully side by side with Slavic Muslims and Catholic Croats. Still, following these loud calls to militant nationalism, Serbian communities living west of the Serbian republic's borders chose to inflict military tragedy on their neighbors rather than to seek rational political dialogue.

Shamelessly exploiting the inherited fear of persecution and massacre (which a huge number of Serbs had, in fact, suffered at the hands of right-wing Croatian nationalist forces during World War II), most, though not all, Belgrade poets sang in synch with populist ideology, igniting Serbian belligerence by calling them "remains of the slaughtered people," deluding them with preposterous, if politically effective, terms of the Serbs as chosen and even "heavenly" people.

Small wonder, then, that in this radically nationalistic tale, all the details of the past stand in service to a single goal: they support the claim that ten years after

Tito's death the time has finally come when Serbia must free herself at last, that the idea and structure of the medieval Serbian kingdom must hold sway wherever Serbian soldiers once set foot.

Sitting in his pillow-strewn bed in the cork-paneled room at Boulevard Haussmann 192, Proust, through contemplating the past, produced a critical anatomy of the *belle époque* in seven books. After reading the anthology of his memories, our own modest ones become more lustrous. Proust's total past invites one to contemplate the necessity of individual and social evolution. Although it develops through fits, sighs, shrieks, whispers, and asides, Proust's nostalgic vision brings us to the redemptive insight that as individuals and as members of a larger society we can assimilate the past only when we accept its totality — when we take upon ourselves the collective's rise and fall, its loathing and grace, its defeats and victories in their entirety.

The *madeleine* became an easily recognizable symbol of involuntary memory because it offered a key to the truth about the past, to that complete web of detail that alone gives shape to the complex tale in which we recognize our own fears and hopes.

In the manipulative hands of yesterday's communists and today's national socialists, the Kosovo peony has been transformed from a symbol of ancient violence against the Serbs into a modern symbol of Serbian violence against all non-Serbs. The Kosovo peony, a fragile flower said to have been born out of Serbian blood spilled centuries ago, has been enthusiastically appropriated in the present-day Serbian state by many para-military organizations and mercenary groups.

The flower's historical message easily lends itself to justification of the current massacres against Bosnians who share with long-gone Ottoman Turks, victors over Serbian knights in the Battle of Kosovo, only the Islamic religion and nothing else. The badges, pins, and tattoos which display the Kosovo peony these days no longer inspire a quiet mourning for deceased medieval heroes of Serbia. Under the murderous hands of Serbian thugs, criminals and bullies, carrying out a perverse revenge for a distant defeat, Kosovo peonies ceased to be a remembrance of Serbs *as* victims. Today, they represent but sorrowful *memento mori* to victims *of* Serbian political madness.

This is why the Balkan war is so shocking to foreign observers. The militant symbolism of the Kosovo peony serves as a mirror only for those whose selective assimilation of history has emboldened them to the greatest brutality.

Wherever collective memory based on the selective use of the past holds sway, everyone thinks alike. When everyone thinks alike, no one thinks at all. A society where no one thinks at all is little more than a frenetic and debauched, if picturesque, village bazaar. It should come as no surprise that those most at home in the crush of this Balkan bazaar are the slave traders, the singers of time-worn songs, the hucksters of dead souls. They vie with each other for the fickle favor of their audience, whose paralyzed fixation on the past allows it to believe only the huckster who pushes his deformed vision of the future the loudest.

The Serbian people have clearly come to listen transfixed to the monotonous song that their baby-faced but politically cunning singer performs on a single string at the threshold of the Bosnian inferno. It is the string of hatred for anyone who does not share the masses' conviction that the Serbian state should extend far beyond the borders it inherited from disintegrated Yugoslavia. The *gusle*, that ancient and simple musical instrument akin to a primitive violin whose quaveringly beautiful accompaniment of the untamed folk imagination cast in decasyllabic verse once enchanted Goethe and the European Romantics, has, in fact, only a single string. And this has made its players all the more determined.

Weaker voices have been drowned out by incessant harangues about "ethnically pure" Serbian territory, and a frustrated Croatian leadership has added similar, if not quite so deafening rumblings to the chorus.

The result? After more than two years of war, the inhabitants of the former Yugoslavia have also come to believe in self-fulfilling prophecies. They are virtually convinced that coexistence in any form had never been possible. Given the endless information war and devastating consequences of Serbia's "just fight," it appears that the history of the former Yugoslavia was, in fact, just a history of waiting for the right moment, when each nation would slam the door shut on its erstwhile neighbors.

If we accept this explanation, then we throw the baby of culture out with the bathwater of politics. If we accept "ethnic cleansing" as a historical necessity, then we forget that Yugoslavia in its best time was a wellspring of diversity and a paragon of admittedly uneasy yet peaceful coexistence.

In spite of today's horror, which is likely to overshadow any recollection of the positive aspects of our life

together, I can still very clearly remember countless instances when our linguistic, artistic, national, and religious differences converged in productive synthesis.

For me, popular slogans about "the celebration of diversity" were never mere philosophical speculation. As far back as I can recall, these differences were the crux of my experience of life at a crossroads of various cultures. When Westerners came to visit, I showed my pride in our federation's diversity with the kind of blissful matter-of-factness that a woodsman shows toward his pine forests, even though their luxuriance is the result of an even succession of dry and rainy days, not any special effort on his part. I considered the diversity of Yugoslav reality to be a fact of nature.

Pathetically but not inaccurately put, Yugoslavia was like a many-colored carpet that allowed me to maintain contact with lands that were dramatically different from the baroque Central European town where I grew up yet still part of the same country.

All those journeys and memories: the chaotic and incredibly lively streets of the Serbian capital city at the confluence of the Sava and Danube rivers, immortalized by the Slovenian romantic poet France Prešeren. There, more than in Istanbul, which leans too far to the East, I realized that the civilizing ethic of the Occident and the Oriental *joie de vivre* converged beautifully in Belgrade.

In Skadarlija, Belgrade's old town, swathed in the smoke of many grills and spits and reverberating with heroic songs from the First World War, I first saw men with unbuttoned shirts and shaggy chests who chewed on sunflower seeds then spat the shells far in front of them onto the sidewalk. For the first time, I sensed the good implicit in the words "vast Slavic soul." This term is so often abused that we Slovenians only grudgingly accept it as applying to us, but our impulsive Serbian cousins can't live without it. My drinking companions feted me, a total stranger, for hours just because they'd learned where I was from. After all, we were all of us "Slavic brothers," weren't we?

Rooted in my memory are the slender minarets of Bosnian villages, where with a mixture of unease and fascination I watched mustachioed men in filigreed vests sitting at outdoor cafés and squinting in the sun, as though they'd walked straight out of Meša Selimovič's brilliant novel *Death and the Dervish*, like the novels of Ivo Andrič an eternal monument to Bosnia. There were Serbian monasteries here, whose gilt frescoes delivered a powerful lesson on the creative force of Eastern Christianity, a force which I later encountered in amazement throughout northern Italy and on the ceilings of San Marco in Venice.

The heavily fortified walls of Dubrovnik defend the independent spirit of the medieval independent republic of Ragusa and the renaissance wisdom of the town motto, *Non bene pro toto libertas venditur auro* (Liberty can by no means be traded for gold.), which the militant savagery of Montenegrin reservists put to a severe test in the 1991-1992 war. The tape of my memory replays the constant hum of Dubrovnik's wide *Stradun*, its main street, in whose shadowy recesses many a summer romance of my generation flowered and faded — Dubrovnik's smooth cobblestone expanses struck us as more conducive to erotic exploration than the plain asphalt of Ljubljana or Zagreb.

For a moment I freely fall victim to the illusion that

I can resurrect the sweet-flowing taste of a watermelon that a couple of affable truck drivers sliced for me once when I was hitchhiking in the Macedonian Vardar River Valley. I was going home to my valley in the Alps, and they were headed even farther, to deliver the produce of their fertile Macedonian fields to market in Western Europe. But we were going in the same direction.

During the ride I learned, much to my amazement, that I wasn't the only one who took so much delight in the variety of Yugoslavia's mosaic. The melodic cadences of those uneducated men bespoke the same sort of pride and fascination. Although we differed from each other in dress, language, religious belief, and taste in music, we had one thing in common: we were familiar strangers. I was more than a thousand kilometers south of my hometown, where, incidentally, some of my truck drivers' friends worked as *Gastarbeiter* (guest workers), spreading the flattering word about the wealthier northern republic to every village in the federation. We paid for our drinks at roadside taverns with the same nearly worthless *dinars*. We had the same kind of passports in our pockets, bound in the same red cover, bearing the same pretentious socialist coat of arms.

One thing that mesmerized me about Macedonia's geography was the faded beauty of Old Skopje, where I sought traces of that spontaneous southern hospitality made famous in one of the most moving elegies in all of the various Yugoslav literatures, *Longing for the South*, the elegy about the sunny lands of childhood that Konstantin Miladinov (1830-1862) wrote from his dreadful exile in Moscow. In a tavern of the same name, I slowly sipped *mastika*, a Macedonian brandy, and meditated on the magnitude of the pain implicit in the loss of a homeland, the psychic displacement of exiles forced into strangers' homes by some absurd resolution of the Communist Information Bureau, the political economy of poverty, or a repressive government. Even as I tried in vain to recite its verses by heart, *Longing for the South* infused me with the bitter sense that the experience of emigration was a crucial part of each of Yugoslavia's distinct cultures.

Never would I have guessed that just ten years after my visit to Skopje, Bosnian, Macedonian, and Serbian friends of mine would experience the pain, if not the words, of that elegy in all the capitals of an indifferent Western Europe — as they hid from the flames of military hell devouring helpless cities like Sarajevo, Goražde, and Mostar; as they fled the Serbian appetite for "Southern Serbia," as Belgrade's architects of carefully designed catastrophe are wont to call Macedonia; and as they evaded conscription into Milošević's army, an army whose officers have killed their own enlisted men when they refused to take part in gang rapes of Moslem women.

On that lazy summer afternoon as I sat wide-eyed and weary-legged in a narrow street in Old Skopje, I couldn't even have dreamed that *Longing for the South* would prove to be so much more than an exercise in romantic poetry — a modern-day prescription for the homesickness that has become the state of mind of so many displaced former Yugoslavs. These days reality has outdone even the wildest nightmares.

Some years later I stopped in at the Chelsea Hotel in New York for a beer. I went there because its

rooms had witnessed America's artistic avant garde at its inception. Because this hotel had offered a roof over the heads of Delmore Schwartz, Lou Reed, Janis Joplin, and Leonard Cohen, I wanted to dip into the aura of that radical adventure that had made American popular culture an integral part of any education in the global village. While I nursed a tepid Rolling Rock, I was struck with a realization long in the making — namely, that I had three powerful forces to thank for the shape of my cultural identity: my native Slovenian tradition, the tradition of worldwide mass culture, and finally the unique experience of Yugoslavia's cultural weaving, which had made my pilgrimage to a café in Skopje as great an existential necessity as my visit to the Chelsea Hotel.

For Macedonian kings of the road it was hardly poetry nor merely the possibility of economic success that drew them to Slovenia. There was also the charm of its difference. As the far northwestern part of Yugoslavia, the former Austro-Hungarian province seemed strange and exotic to these descendants of Ottoman vassals, and yet it was part of the same country that they lived in.

The most exotic things are close at hand. The Freudian concept of *das Unheimliche* really applies to those seldom-noticed eccentricities in our everyday world that, when observed, hold the greatest fascination of all. And this was precisely the dimension of our Yugoslav being which led, in its extreme form, to the violent disintegration of the federal state. Maintaining a life in tension between your native culture and foreign ones is doubtlessly exhausting since it forces you to examine the validity of your own assumptions. But that is the only productive way. Whenever we try to eliminate the tension, it comes back with a vengeance. As Belgrade aspired to absolute power, the differences between its national socialist politics and the other republics gradually became intolerable.

The Serbian inability to accept differences reared its Medusa's head in Kosovo, long before the outbreak of war. The apartheid that the Serbian regime has been using for more than a decade to break the spirit of ethnic Albanians who have lived there for centuries has its roots in the conviction that Serbian culture alone is possessed of great qualities. While bullets ricochet over Albanian rooftops and the Serbian minority drives them out of their walled compounds with fire and sword, Belgrade's propaganda machine belches forth an endless string of insults that denies the Albanian Kosovars their very humanity, reducing them to the status of animals fit to be shot. The Kosovars have thus become an instrument of evil: "Islamic fundamentalists," a "demographic time-bomb," "uncivilized scum." Only with the elimination of the evil and foreign element from the nation's body will the Serbian people at last be free, shout the little Serbian Goebbelses.

The brutal treatment of the Kosovars offered Belgrade a convenient formula for its belligerent relations with other non-Serbs. From this paranoid perspective, everyone becomes a subversive foreigner: the Slovenians are "lackeys of Vienna," the Croats are "genocidal *ustaša*," Bosnians are Moslemized Serbs or Islamic *mujaheddin*, the West is convulsing in the clutches of a "Vatican conspiracy and the Fourth Reich." And so on. You may continue the list at random; the basic model is there. Whatever is unusual, different, or foreign merits contempt, expulsion, death. The differences that once made Yugoslavia a paragon of Europe's cultural richness have vanished irrevocably in the winds of war.

II.

"Brush Me With Your Knee
Beneath the Table . . ."

I admit: thanks to lucky circumstances and the effective resistance of the Slovenian territorial defense force in the Ten Day War against the Serb-dominated Yugoslav army, I didn't have to go into exile. Even so, I grieve for my lost South on a metaphysical level that has nothing to do with our former governmental structure.

My grief for the South nurtures no nostalgia for the centralized politics of Belgrade. No, my grief for the South catches instead occasional hints of the intoxicating scent of flowering plum trees in a Bosnian orchard. It speaks in the shrill cries of half-tame cormorants on Macedonia's Lake Dojran. It is reflected in the crystalline blueness of a cave on the Croatian island of Biševo, which in beauty far exceeds the much better-known Grotta Azzura on the Island of Capri. If Andre Gide had truly wanted to escape from there, he would certainly have discovered a domain of sea gods in the deep blue waters of Biševo.

My grief for the South softly hums the Dalmatian love songs that we Slovenian schoolboys preferred to the melancholy folk songs of our own republic near the Alps. My grief for the South thumbs through the private lexicon of Belgrade literary societies, now exiled, but which used to witness debates about Derrida and Rilke and passionate discussions about the historical novels of Serbian writer Miloš Crnjanski and the unsettling tales of Slovenian writer Drago Jančar. It fumbles for expression in some long-forgotten alcoholic stupor on the waterfront of Split, the Dalmatian coastal town in which Italian and Croatian languages mingle seamlessly. It sways in a half-smoked joint rolled from grass grown by an acquaintance on the island of Vis.

My grief for the South murmurs the lyrics of Johnny Štulić, the lead singer and guitarist of the legendary rock band *Azra*, cheered on at concerts in every part of the former Yugoslavia by multitudes of enthusiastic teenagers, myself included. Although he sang in Croatian about the same things as Lou Reed, his raspy voice was just as consistently his own, expressing an individuality now verging on superfluous in this age of the rule of army boots. He was an enemy of fads, and trendy posturing was alien to him. This is why we felt so close to him. He didn't promise the Kingdom of Heaven on earth; instead, he portrayed the world as a Swedenborgian hell wearing the mask of heavenly idols.

When he sang of late-night wanderings through labyrinths of dimly lit city streets and described people made into targets of hatred because of their membership in one or another minority, he always proceeded from the fundamental conviction that the easiest choice is also the worst, and that you have to back your words up with your life. When, as a high school student, I saw him for the first time in the auditorium of Memorial Hall in Ljubljana, I distinctly felt that I was watching a prophet.

His message of faithfulness to self and anarchic freedom was immediately understood by a whole generation of young Yugoslavs who may have prayed to different gods but who worshiped one and the same prophet, the prophet of rock and roll.

Once, long ago, when I was wandering through the Kornati archipelago in the Adriatic Sea, I came across a grafitto on an island so remote that it was serviced by a boat from the mainland only twice a week. Scrawled across the stuccoless wall of a village tavern, it didn't proclaim apocalyptic platitudes about the monumental loss of meaning, the way grafitti do today. Instead, its crude characters conveyed a gospel of love. My heart jumped, its beat quickened.

I was devoted to Yugo-rock because I sought an authentic way of being that would bring me close to people who could understand joy and sadness without a lot of unnecessary words. Here, on this craggy forsaken island in the midst of the Adriatic, I discovered a kindred spirit who in one short sentence expressed my enthusiasm for the rock singer who had hauntingly translated our intimate dilemmas into soul-shaking music. The message read: Štulic is god. That was all I needed. I had come home.

The passion that Johnny Štulić invested in his songs about the bitter pain and miraculous hope of social outcasts was a passion to bear witness. For those of us crowding around the stage, that passion broke through the layers of our adolescent mannerisms and became a document of vulnerability that allowed an entire generation of young Yugoslavs to discover themselves in Štulić's lyrics. It was powerful and prescient testimony about the fate of a world that the gods had abandoned and that man was also trying to forsake.

Yugo-rock never wanted to conceal its flirtation with shepherds' songs or the Macedonian panpipes that our rock musicians' mothers had listened to as they worked the fields. Of course, Yugo-rock was based on the universal configuration of bass, guitar, drums, and voice, but it also drew on the living wellsprings of southern Slavic folk melodies.

The result: while our Western contemporaries were practicing standard numbers like "Yellow Submarine" and "Rock 'n' Roll Music," novice guitarists in basements and garages all over Yugoslavia tried to imitate the seven-eighths rhythms of Bosnian blues immortalized immortal by the vertiginously popular Sarajevo band *White Button* in songs like "Selma," "Don't Sleep, My Sweet," and "Blame it on the Bad Wine," which provided my schoolmates and me with unforgettable anthems to sing in the corridors of Sarajevo First High School, Zagreb Classical, and Ljubljana-Šentvid High Schools in the equally amateurish way as we marked the passing of our youth.

The etymological sense of *amateur* stems from "love for the thing itself." Our limited pleasure in the imperfect product of that love may after all have been the only conceivable reward for our faithfulness to the common, if frail, mentality that was inspired by the cultures of Central Europe, the Balkans, the Mediterranean, and the Pannonian plain.

I am convinced that Yugo-rock afforded me the rare chance to live in a multicultural society long before that term was co-opted as the official protective coloring

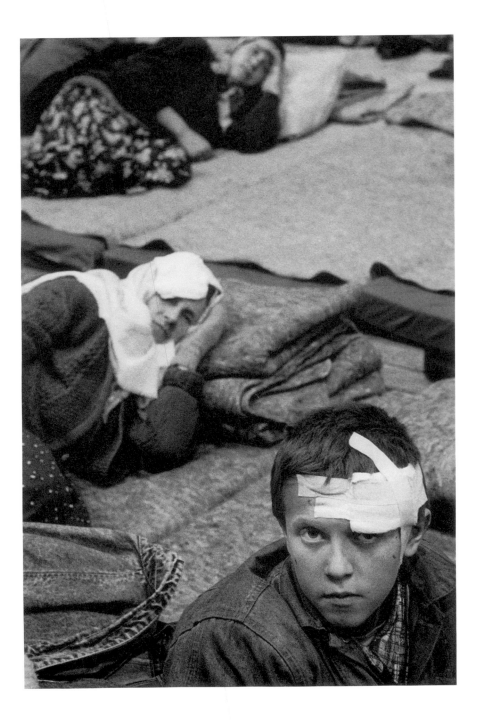

of the politically correct.

On my way home from the United States soon after the outbreak of the present Balkan war, I stopped over in Paris. As I waited for a metro train, I could hear echoing through the chilly underground station a familiar melody from another time, another world. I was pulled toward its source, gently and irresistibly.

A dark-haired, young man of woeful demeanor, with a crumpled cap laying inverted on the floor in front of him, was playing the guitar as he stared fixedly ahead. None of the other passers-by bothered to stop. Why should they?

But I shuddered, recognizing in a split-second the lyrical ballad that had once helped me express the pain of a young, broken heart. I was instantly seized with a sharp, yet graceful, nostalgia, inundated by a flood of emotion, while the unschooled singer's voice eerily reverberated off the subway station walls. Listen, listen carefully to the song that my unhappy countryman sang:

> Somebody loves me
> dreams about me
> casts furtive glances
> but I don't know who
> somebody loves me
> when I go roaming
> crossing the street
> same as me
> I study the faces
> examine the crowd
> somebody looks for me
> I don't know where

somebody loves me
gives me their soul
someone's a stranger here
same as me
the neon light's shadow
grows longer
the longing in your eyes
gives you away
tonight you can ask around
for me again
put your hands in your pockets
and walk away.

In his *Biographia Literaria* Coleridge writes that "it is not the poem that we have read, but the one to which we return that possesses true power." I am not the only one who keeps turning to the unmistakable sentiment in Štulić's lyric "People of Loneliness." All of us do who desperately keep seeking an understanding companion at train stations, airports, in the world's waiting rooms — someone who has undergone the same rites of passage that took place all over the former Yugoslavia in one and the same rhythm, by dint of the fact that we listened ecstatically to the same rock singers and read the same poets. The names of these singers and poets remained unpronounceable anywhere in Western Europe, but for us they embodied the flickering light in a tunnel of political obscurantism.

If you don't realize what you've lost, then you've lost nothing. I know very well what I have lost: the experience of that singularly rich identity — the product of a unique, challenging, yet uncommonly charming cosmos

— to Belgrade's military ambitions. Deprived of the lark's song above the Sora River's floodplain in Slovenia, thunderstorms over the Karst, or the soundless flow of minerals in the sharp-edged Julian Alps, that cosmos would be just as impoverished as my youth would have been had there been no rock music, no books or friendships to anchor us in what was a broader Yugoslav community.

I am convinced that rock music will never be the same for me, thanks to Yugoslavia's violent disintegration. It wasn't just the proverbial wisdom of the Beatles and a wailing Mick Jagger that I grew up with; just as important were the original songs by *White Button*, the *Idols* from Belgrade, *Bread and Salt* from Macedonia, and a host of other bands whose half-forgotten names once signified a genuine sentimental education for the generation that long ago, oh, so long ago, turned out in the tens of thousands for Yugoslavia's first Woodstock in a village outside of Belgrade. That experience led us to believe — naively — that the good vibrations of our collective transcendence would mark a new life in harmony, like stars, like the four seasons.

The guns of the Balkan war have silenced those good vibrations. Yugo-rock stars have dispersed among the four corners of the earth. The stars have set. And of all seasons the lands south of my new country know but a single one — the deep, dark winter of death.

My throat constricts and I grow tense when I quietly mourn for the South. Still, the first gunshot of the war for Slovenia made it absolutely clear to me that this sorrow is rooted in the depths of an irrevocable past. Czeslaw Milosz captures that state ineffably in one melancholy line of his *Elegy for N.N.*: "And the heart doesn't die when one thinks it should." Because the heart has its reasons, of which the mind has no understanding, the metaphysics of my divided heart still grow from the memory of a shared past that I cannot renounce.

Hordes of arrogant officers and drunken reservists have annexed the *Heimat* — that social, national, and political construct of one's home. But we, eternal children, refuse to have our *Heim* taken away, the only refuge left to us: our imaginary community, the private spaces of our memory, the river flowing under the Three Bridges in Ljubljana, dim stars over Škrlatica Mountain, the faces of loved ones, blossoming magnolias, chalk-white paths in a city park, or the pain of an irretrievable past.

Yet I'm fully aware that the past of my memory has no connection to the present. I became convinced of this during ten days in the short, hot summer of 1991 that may not have changed the world but that marked the beginning of a new era for me and my countrymen. In the midst of the ten-day war for Slovenia, as Yugoslav tanks encircled the capital city of my country, I walked down the eerily empty streets of a Ljubljana suburb to visit my parents and sister.

Together with other residents of their small apartment building, they were holing out in the basement, a space that had never before served its original purpose. Instead of the bomb shelter equipped for survival that one was supposed to have expected — given the all-pervasive paranoia about possible attacks by the West that Tito carefully cultivated to maintain control of his communist empire — this basement had never been anything

but a storage area: rough-hewn shelves along the walls, discarded camping tables and well-worn chairs on the floor, all brought here by the thriftiness of my parents, who had experienced the "seven lean years" of post-war Yugoslavia as young adults.

The shelves had warped under the weight of many jars of home-grown pickles, tomatoes, and plum preserves. Bottles of deep-red Karst wine, *teran*, glinted dustily; under them were heaps of discarded newspapers. Next to a road bike stood a pair of racing skis. In the far corner was a huge, old-fashioned cabinet containing the magazines and books that I had bought as a student at Ljubljana University and deposited in the basement's dank treasure house before I left for the United States.

A radio announcer's assuring voice reminded us that we should take food and identification papers with us into the shelters. The rattle of automatic weapons fire echoed faintly from the city center. Slovenian militiamen were trying to take out Yugoslav Army snipers disguised as civilians, some of whom would escape, later to perfect their murderous craft at the windows of Sarajevo's high-rises. The air quavered in the summer heat, wailing sirens warned of a possible air raid, a dog padded through front yards dragging his leash behind him: the place was deserted.

War, I thought countless times in those few days. This is really war. Not the war of movies about the glorious partisan days, with Richard Burton as a young Marshal Tito leading his divisions out of a German trap in *Sutieska* (1973), an overblown two-hour epic about the legendary battle that we schoolboys reenacted to exhaustion on dusty playgrounds. This was a real war, where children whined in bomb shelters, their parents gazed fear-ridden into the darkness, and my colleagues found that the unrestrainable urge to defend their home suddenly transformed them from warehousemen, computer experts, and students of economics into commited fighters.

Happy to see each other again, my sister, mother, father and I embraced. Words were superfluous. To touch each other was enough. This was the most important thing: before the Ten-Day War, I had never realized so clearly that my life is so excruciatingly linked to that of my loved ones.

Even though Slovenia experienced the war in a relatively mild form, it brought us something we never would have been able to attain in peace. The immediate threat of bodily harm intensifies one's metaphysical awareness of that love about which Denis de Rougement says in his book *Les mythes de l'amour* (1961) that "only because of love is something the way it is, that form and motion exist thanks to it, both the nearby and the far away, the world and the individual, desire, suffering, and joy." The pain of the possibility of losing a loved one became an integral part of one's fatefully altered perception of the world.

In disbelief my sister tested the clasps of the flak jacket I had been wearing as a field interpreter for CNN, while I stepped over to the rustic cabinet and slowly opened its rickety doors.

What I saw was an unforgettable vision of grieving for the South. A panorama of Yugoslavia's intellectual profile opened up before me — that Yugoslavia into which I'd been born and which I had loved, but in whose name Belgrade's generals were now unblinkingly ready to level entire cities and reduce whole villages to dust. I stood there, dumbstruck and shaken. From the trenches where Slovenian soldiers fought against the Yugoslav Army, against officers and peach-fuzzed enlisted men from Kosovo and Montenegro, Macedonia and the Serbian highlands, the sarcasm of history had brought me to this cellar, to this old peasant cupboard stuffed from top to bottom with books in all the major languages of the former Yugoslavia, books that had formed not just my academic and literary career, but my personality itself.

Here were slender paperbacks from the *Word and Thought* series that introduced me as an eighteen-year-old to the sensual world of Persian poetry in Serbian translation. Next to them were the penetrating essays of Czeslaw Milosz, his *Visions from San Francisco Bay*; later, in New York, I would compare the deluxe cover design of the American edition with the modest and economical design of my Serbian translation, which had won its Vojvodinian publisher the allegiance of a generation of grateful young readers. The compendious works of Averroes, Plotinus and Aristotle gathered dust in one Zagreb publisher's characteristic, pale yellow jackets, from which I could immediately recognize a philosophy student's apartment, whether I was staying overnight with acquaintances in Niš, Ohrid, or Vinkovci.

Here were issues of the Macedonian literary magazine *Young Fighter*, in which I'd aspired to publish as a beginning poet. Volumes of Bachelard's reveries on the poetics of space and Benjamin's *Moscow Diary*, both pub-

lished in Sarajevo in exotic-sounding Serbo-Croatian —
thanks to the Bosnian translator's penchant for drawing
on both Serbian and Croatian lexicons — with the
faintest hint of a muezzin's call to prayer in the sentence
melody. Brodsky, Lautreaumont, Tsvetaeva, and
Mandelstam, all of whom I discovered in Serbian translation in unprepossessing little white paperbacks that I
bought in bookstores in both Novi Sad and Ljubljana. A
collection of poems by my friend Tomaž Šalamun that
came out in translation in Montenegro.

The entire first year's installment of a prestigious
series of the world's hundred best novels in Slovenian
translation and lovingly crafted bindings, half-buried
under old issues of the Belgrade magazine *Literary News*
and *Quorum* from Zagreb, where for several years I had
my own poetics column and my own regular translator. A
Description of Death, a book of short stories by the Serbian
Jewish writer David Albahari with a friendly dedication
from the author. Stack after stack of miscellaneous literary reviews, almanacs, anthologies with versions of my
work by various translators in various languages, a slew
of collections and little magazines to which I had enthusiastically contributed as poet or essayist before they
either died or were consumed in the widening abyss of
nationalist exclusivism.

Out of the gentle swirls of dust from the yellowed
spines of books and the pages turned a hundred times,
out of the imaginative tales in which I lost myself so
many times — with the passion of a reader by vocation
and conviction without really being aware of what language I was reading in, Slovenian or Serbo-Croatian, in
which I was almost as fluent as in my native language

thanks to many visits to the South — from the fading faces of the editors, writers, and translators with whom I associated at major literary festivals and informal chamber readings from Cetinje to Sarajevo, from Bled to Struga; out of these hazy images arose a fragile web of close personal friendships that truly knew no national or language barriers. These friendships had been born in the sweet vacuum of eternity to which only the tragic muse of art can deliver us; and we stubbornly believed in that muse, for we were incapable of believing in any of the Great Ideas.

• • •

Throughout the time I was growing up — the late 1970s and early '80s — I shared with my peers the easy feeling that we didn't have it bad at all. We were different from our counterparts in the Soviet empire's East European satellites by way of the nonaligned politics of Tito, the great guru of the "third way," who discovered the trick of playing West and East off each other so that both sides would generously contribute money to build his Potemkin villages of self-management. But those were issues of high diplomacy that for a long time we neither understood nor cared about. Our interests lay elsewhere.

Most of all, we wanted to know in what European town Oscar Peterson would be playing next summer and when John Fowles's newest book would hit the bookstores in nearby Trieste, Vienna, or Munich, if not Ljubljana. We traveled widely and unhindered, both within Yugoslavia and abroad. We made pilgrimages to jazz and rock concerts as far afield as Moers, Florence, and

Montreux. We believed that mass culture gave us more in common with youth in London than with our parents. In their novels and literary reviews, our older colleagues had told unsettling stories of suffering in the clutches of Titoism, of the communist regime's brutality, but we understood these then as a far-removed allegory that no longer defined us in any significant way.

Because we lived in an apocryphal ghetto on the edge of history's real currents, from which we hoped to glimpse man's contradictions more clearly, it was not difficult for us to turn down offers to join in the growing din of public hysteria that began to proclaim its grand plans of Nation and Statehood in the 1980s. Our older colleagues turned into public dissidents whose Minervan owls were now taking flight even in broad daylight.

Yet we remained convinced we were living in a world that didn't interest us, commited to the lost cause that was our home. Because we were no longer the babbling step-children of Coca-Cola and Marx, but rather their uncertain hostages, we grew even more inspired by the modest pleasures of lonely people living in barren rooms, and our writing became the quandary of describing those lives. We were desperate to gain the muses' favor in an ambitious, if precariously elusive, project — to get the angels of private life and the demons of history to glimpse each other just once in the mirror of everyday banality.

Of course, this was not a time of absolute freedom. Still, society *was* open for public debate. In contrast to the Stalinist times that preceded ours, there were virtually no ideological taboos, no censors looking over our shoulders. The blacklists of forbidden authors had all but disappeared. This is why the external need to write Aesopian tales and in coded metaphors vanished as well. Young writers in Zagreb, Ljubljana, and Belgrade were independently coming to the same tenuous conclusion: our priority lay in personal mythologies and the existential drama between I and thou.

We knew intuitively that the artist could speak of his own spirit, and thus indirectly about the spirit of the historical age, only from the margins of his society. The bound volumes of the Slovenian magazine *Literatura*, the Croatian *Quorum*, and the Serbian *Literary Word* were packed with poems and stories, each of which is a minor proof of the belief that the literature we wrote in the '80s was one extended metaphor for the courage to be — to be oneself beyond all national ideologies, political parties, and historical programs.

Dissatisfied with an atmosphere in which dissident books were praised precisely for the sharpness of their critical insight regardless of aesthetic standards, we set out on the strenuous path of depoliticizing literature. On the pages of *Quorum*, especially, we stressed over and over that if one or the other moral stance is already evident from the allegories of history and the metaphors of everyday speech, there should be no need to emphasize that moral stance for special effect.

In the course of the '80s, *Quorum* served as fire to the moths of our literary visions, which flew only at night and cautiously, for our poems were heeded only by those who shared our belief that in order to speak competently about the world outside, one must first look into the murky pools of one's own psyche. Writing in the anonymous highrises of Novi Beograd, in the garrets of

Zagreb's Upper Town, or in the old bourgeois row houses of Ljubljana, we may indeed have argued passionately about the meaning of metafiction and the styles of radical will, but we were united in one fundamental conviction — that the poet's task to recognize his historical circumstances grows out of the use of language and local tradition.

For Western readers avid for dissidents, this shift of focus diluted the usual romanticized East European drama of writer versus censor. But at the price of a smaller reading audience, we gained the freedom to write lyrical meditations whose tiny flame had to be protected time and again from the fierce winds of a *poésie engagé*.

We did not reinvent the wheel. But we sensed that by defending our introspective verses we were in a way defending the very idea of freedom. The social prestige of an ever-growing army of hacks, whose impoverished imaginations were the currency of their short-lived political fame, constantly forced us to respond to the cheap reproach that we were escaping from reality, that we were retreating into infinite cosmologies and philosophical paradoxes in the style of Borges's short stories, the popularity of which had condemned a whole generation of young Yugoslav writers to the pejorative epithet "Borgesian."

The truly decisive role in our formation as writers, however, wasn't Borges, as influential as he was, but the Serbian-Jewish writer Danilo Kiš. History and the individual mirror each other in his stories with a distinct longing for existential mystery that was far more telling to those of us living in a land where peace was just the short interval between wars than the timeless labyrinth of the

Argentinian's inventions could ever be. More than in *Aleph* or *The Garden of Forking Paths*, we sought in *A Tomb for Boris Davidovich*, *Early Sorrows*, and *The Encyclopedia of the Dead* potent hints for freeing ourselves from the the demands of an often pedagogical literature in which the writer's one and only function was to be a pillar of civic courage.

Fortunately, we had learned from observing our own troubled societies that the forces of good and evil were not neatly separated by the line dividing communists from noncommunists, compelling us to see that complex reality required an equally complex literary response. In this way Central and Eastern Europe witnessed a shift in the use of poetry, which too often had been fraught with an exalted political or moral "noble mind" which has, as Czeslaw Milosz once shrewdly observed, no place in poems.

Small wonder, then, that we young Slovenian writers took a Joycean stance of *non serviam* toward the cause of Slovenia's independence during the '80s; yet during the Ten-Day War we immediately responded to the call of civic responsibility. In accordance with our philosophy of political abstinence, we set literature aside and demonstrated our unambiguous existential commitment in TV and radio reports, newspaper columns, and even in the ranks of the territorial militia.

Our older colleagues had won much-deserved applause by using critical distance and the merciless scalpel of truth to expose "socialism with a human face" for what it was. Our aesthetic imagination, however, had been shaped by a different theater. We summoned our creative talents around a problem that may not have been publicly attractive but was, and continues to be, privately challenging. Instead of socialism and its spectacular burial, we focused on the scars, nicks, creases, and grimaces on the faces of individuals. We felt our way around the depths of the human soul in the agonized silence during a wake, when the reign of death begins to relent but hasn't yet vanished altogether and the soul can so easily stray amid the shadows of paranoia and anxiety.

The poet can give testimony to his time only if his metaphors are freed from external necessity, regardless of the ideological camp where they originate. This was our tenet, and we kept repeating this minor revelation in all the languages of what was once Yugoslavia. But it did not mean that our "generation without charismatic mentors," as it was often called in the press, closed its eyes to the social and historical reality around it.

The opposite was instead true. Writing ordinary stories about ordinary people, we tried to reveal the consequences that social changes had for the individuals' way of feeling and thinking, for their dire need and their tiny joys. In the temporary residence of that ghetto where we felt at home thanks to our mutual support and elective affinities, out of our individual efforts to capture in words that dark world in which none of us would wish to live, but must live nonetheless, grew the collective — erotic, almost — dedication to literature and a certain cultural mentality to which I contributed during the 1980s.

At the precise moment when tanks began rolling out of the garrisons outside Ljubljana to forcefully maintain the collective state at any cost, the political idols of the Yugoslav experiment were dashed to pieces. The

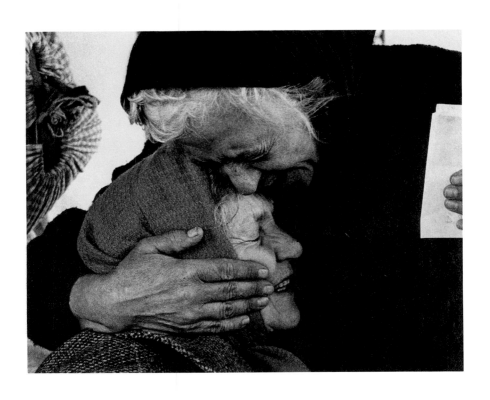

masks fell. Now, uniformed criminals dance, torrents of nameless refugees rush toward an uncertain future. The tidal wave of unrestrained militarism gains momentum. The flags of local warlords flutter higher on their staffs each day. The world begins to crumble like stale bread.

In a cramped room on East Eleventh Street in New York's Lower East Side sits a group of students and engineers, architects and poets who until yesterday had lived in a single state but who today have different countries. A worn-out record plays on the stereo. A Serb from Croatia, a famous stage performer from a country that no longer exists, recorded this selection of popular chansons long before the invention of laser disk technology.

Outside, the capital city of the twentieth century noisily goes about its business. But we lean forward and hold our breath, the better to soak up this old song of a Croatian poet. Rade Šerbedžija sings it with the soft and gentle voice of someone who has no inkling that one day this crackling record's melancholy message will offer its listeners the only available substitute for a home. They know that Theodor von Adorno was right when he wrote in his essay on Heinrich Heine that homelessness has become our fate, that both our language and our being are damaged by exile.

Some of us went overseas into voluntary exile years before the Balkan War with vague longing for a personal change but with the redemptive knowledge that we could always return to our newly independent republic at the foothills of the Alps, which the dragon of war has barely brushed with its tail. With our less fortunate friends from the devastated regions of the former Yugoslavia, however, we share an unpleasant feeling that we live the Heineesque lives of people who are looking for the way home. We keep hopefully looking for the place that was existentially real for us in the same way that childhood alone is real for the artist.

The childhood of the South Slavs' life in a common state is lost forever, and we listen all the more intently to this performance of a song that we've heard a hundred times before, and though it was written about an individual, the unexpected twists of history now reveal in it a metaphor of our collective fate.

> Don't give in to the years, Inez,
> . . . brush me with your knee beneath the table,
> my generation, my love.

A friend sitting next to me on a threadbare couch begins to sob. A tiny, almost invisible, stream runs down her cheeks, which suggest age beyond her years. Her tears are a sign that our shared experience of this sentimental song — with which boys in provincial capitals from the Alps to the Vardar used to court their girls — has now become a key to our elective affinity. Thus, those "beautiful moments of nostalgia, love, and loneliness," as the song goes, are not an ephemeral historical document but a magic formula that secures our passage to that refuge among the eternally young landscapes of the spirit in which we will always be at home.

Ljubljana - New York
July 1993

Notes

The Photographs

Cover: Sarajevo, Bosnia - Zlad and Admir Selimbegovic, Muslim refugees and brothers from a village outside Sarajevo, walk arm in arm by a bombed out department store on Zrinjskog Street in Sarajevo.

Page 15: Mostar, Bosnia - Destruction across the Neretva River in Mostar in February, 1993.

Page 21: Karlovac, Croatia - A Bosnian Muslim refugee from Prijedor prays next to her bunk bed in Karlovac Ex-detainee center, a refugee center for Bosnians who were once prisoners in Serbian detention camps.

Page 27: Sarajevo, Bosnia - Refugee children in a makeshift shelled school in Sarajevo.

Page 33: Sarajevo, Bosnia - A woman washes her laundry in the Bosna River in Sarajevo. For most Sarajevans, washing machines sat idle throughout the war becaue of lack of running water.

Page 39: Tuzla, Bosnia - A mother and son from the besieged enclave of Srebenica during their first hours as refugees in Tuzla.

Page 51: Tuzla, Bosnia - A wounded boy from Srebenica in the Tuzla Sport Center after riding on the back of U.N. trucks to escape his beseiged city.

Page 57: Sarajevo, Bosnia - Sele Sokobovic, the guitarist for a young Sarajevan band called "Panic Noise," plays an original song as friends listen and sing along. Sele and his other band members converted a basement storage room into their practicing room so they could continue to play as Sarajevo was shelled by Serbian nationalists.

Page 63: Sarajevo, Bosnia - Two Sarajevan children, Irena and Adnan, in their Bosnian army uniforms, which they crafted from tent canvas. Twelve-year-old Irena explains that she wears her uniform daily and carries her fake gun to show solidarity with the Bosnian army fighters who defend her city.

Page 71: Gasinci, Croatia - Two Bosnian women, who spent their lives as neighbors in the same Bosnian village, embrace as they say farewell. One is Muslim, the other Catholic. Refugees for six months in the same refugee center in Croatia, they were finally forced to separate as part of a Croatian government's new policy of ethnic and religious segregation of refugees. On this day, buses arrived to take the Catholic refugees to a separate center.

AUSTRIA
Karavanke
Bled
Ljubljana
SLOVENIA
Zagreb
CROATIA
Sava
HUNGARY
Danube
Vukovar
Vinkovci
VOJVODINA
Novi Sad
Belgrade
ROMANIA
BOSNIA
HERCEGOVINA
Sarajevo
Mostar
YUGOSLAVIA
Niš
Adriatic
Solit
Biševo
Vis
Dubrovnik
MONTENEGRO
Cetinje
KOSOVO
ITALY
Sea
BULGARIA
Skopje
MACEDONIA
Vardar
Struga
Ohrid
Dojran Lake
ALBANIA
GREECE

Countries that Emerged
out of Disintegrated Yugoslavia
in 1991

Map design by Vida Ogorelec.

The Author

Aleš Debeljak is considered by critics to be one of the premier poets of Central Europe. He received his doctorate in social thought from Syracuse University and has held writing fellowships from both the Virginia Center for the Creative Arts and Cambridge University.

He has published five books of poetry, the most recent being *Anxious Moments* (White Pine Press, 1994) and three books of cultural criticism. He edited the Slovenian, Croatian and Serbian section of *Shifting Borders: East European Poetries in the '80s* (Farleigh Dickinson University Press, 1993) and was editor of *Prisoners of Freedom: Contemporary Slovenian Poetry* (Pedernal Press, 1994). His numerous awards include the Prešeren Prize, which is the Slovenian National Book Award, and the Hayden Carruth Poetry Prize.

His work frequently appears in literary journals in the United States. *Twilight of the Idols* has been published in German, Croatian, Hungarian, Polish, and Czech.

The Photographer

Born in Boston, Massachusetts, in 1966, Elizabeth Rappaport studied political science and photography at Cornell University, New York, receiving her B.A. in 1989. She has traveled extensively through Eastern Europe working for national and international publications and humanitarian organizations. In 1993 and 1994 she made numerous trips to the former Yugoslavia. She has exhibited her work resulting from these trips in solo and group exhibitions throughout the United States. She currently lives in Colorado and is affiliated with J. B. Pictures of New York.

The Translator

Michael Biggins has translated widely from Slovene and Russian, with work appearing in *Grand Street*, *Paris Review*, *Ploughshares*, and elsewhere. He lives in Lawrence, Kansas.